Original title:
Sapling's Song

Copyright © 2025 Creative Arts Management OÜ
All rights reserved.

Author: Vivian Laurent
ISBN HARDBACK: 978-1-80567-062-9
ISBN PAPERBACK: 978-1-80567-142-8

The Young Tree's Harmonious Journey

In a pot, I dream of height,
With a gnome who sings at night.
Leaning left, I lose my grip,
A leaf falls off, I start to slip.

Sunbeams tickle my green cheek,
Squirrels dance while I just peek.
I stretch out wide, a leafy star,
"I'm just a tree," I shout—how bizarre!

Symphony of the Flourishing Foliage

Among the boughs, a bug does hum,
A critter choir—oh, what a strum!
The ants march in with tiny feet,
Demanding snacks, a leafy treat.

A gust of wind, I sway and bend,
The neighbors gaze, is this the end?
I chuckle soft, will I take flight?
Don't worry, folks, I'll stand upright!

Ode to the Earth's Tender Beginnings

From acorn small to leafy feast,
Insects gather like a feast!
Caterpillars wriggle by,
While I just laugh and wave goodbye.

My branches tickle passing dreams,
As sunlight drizzles through the beams.
I giggle as the sparrows sing,
Who knew that growing could be a fling?

The Fresh Whisper of the Forest

Beneath my shade, a picnic sprawls,
While ants parade and nature calls.
A butterfly plays peek-a-boo,
I roll my eyes, "What will you do?"

With every gust, I sway and bend,
The garden party will not end.
Let's sing and dance, no need for stress,
Being a tree is such a mess!

Breaths of the Youngest Oak

In the breeze, a giggle flows,
As tiny leaves wave, nobody knows.
Each sprout a dancer in sunlight's play,
Chasing shadows that wiggle away.

Roots twist like fingers in hide-and-seek,
Whispering secrets, but oh, how they squeak!
Bugs join the chorus, a silly tune,
Bouncing on branches, they sway to the moon.

Notes of Flourishing Foliage

The branches hum with laughter bright,
Tickling the clouds, oh, what a sight!
Leaves gossip softly like best friends do,
While squirrels play tag—who's the fastest crew?

A tickle from raindrops makes them giggle,
As lightning bugs dance, their bellies wiggle.
The sun winks down with a cheeky grin,
Nature's comedy show is about to begin!

The Canvas of Spring's Awakening

Sprouts pop up like jokes on a page,
Each petal a punchline, bursting with gage.
The grass tickles toes, a soft, silly jest,
While flowers compete in a colorful quest.

Worms wiggle in rhythm, a wacky parade,
Painting the ground in nature's charade.
With every bloom, there's laughter anew,
Spring's canvas is vibrant, and silly too!

Nature's First Harmonies

The robins chirp in a comical choir,
Rhythms of nature, they never tire.
Wind joins in with a merry twirl,
Whipping the blossoms in a playful whirl.

Silly ants march, in perfect sync,
Filling their baskets, but what do they think?
Nature's own sitcom, a riotous spree,
With every flap, there's more to see!

Sprints in Nature's Orchestra

In the garden, roots take flight,
Chasing bugs in morning light.
With a twist and little spin,
They laugh and giggle, where to begin!

Worms do leap like bouncy balls,
While daisies dance, they heed the calls.
Rabbits hop—oh what a sight!
Nature's band, all feeling bright!

A breeze comes in, and grass sways,
They sing for hours, in playful ways.
On every sprout, a secret hum,
In this concert, fun is when they come!

So with the wind, their tunes they share,
A waltz of leaves fills the fresh air.
Roots and shoots in joyful glee,
Life's garden party—come join the spree!

Whispers of Young Roots

Little roots in the damp ground,
Whisper secrets, oh what a sound!
They tickle the soil, giggling low,
Sharing tales of where they'll go.

"I'm stretching wide!" one root proclaims,
"Bet I can reach where sunlight flames!"
"Not if I tangle and pull you back!"
They cheer and tease in a playful pack.

Ants march by, carrying crumbs,
And roots laugh out, "Hey, here comes the fun!"
With each tiny wiggle, they take their stand,
Whispers of joy through all of the land.

When rain drops fall and slip away,
They chatter loudly, dance and sway.
"More water please!" they shout with glee,
A merry tune from roots so free!

Echoes of Green Dreams

In the meadow where green dreams play,
Tiny sprouts laugh and sway.
"Look at us, so small yet bold,
With sunshine stories waiting to be told!"

The grass whispers jokes to hungry bees,
While petals chuckle in the breeze.
Each flower blushes a vibrant hue,
As seeds conspire what next to do!

"Shall we leap like frogs?" one cheekily vows,
"Or play dress-up in leafy brows?"
With laughter rippling like the stream,
They bounce along in a joyful dream.

"Catch the clouds, let's see them race!"
A game of tag in a sunny space.
With every giggle, the garden beams,
Echoing joy in green dreams!

The Melody of New Leaves

New leaves croon in a rustling choir,
Broken branches, their hearts on fire.
"Swing me high, let's catch a breeze!"
They sway and twist with giggling ease.

A woodland laugh here, a chuckle there,
Each leaf jests like a fresh pair.
"Hey watch me twirl! Look at my spin!"
In their merry dance, happiness begins.

Sudden showers make them glide,
In puddles bright, they take a ride.
"Watch out for splashes!" they tease and hoot,
In this watery fun, they never lose hope!

As dusk draws near, their song grows light,
Whispered laughter fades into night.
They rest in dreams, a leafy throng,
Spreading joy with every song!

The Harmonic Journey of New Life

From tiny seed to sprouting green,
A rubbery dance, quite a scene.
Wiggly worms join in the spree,
Singing loud in harmony.

With crispy leaves that flop and sway,
They catch the breeze in a playful way.
Their laughter tickles the sunny sky,
Making all the birds pass by.

Roots are tangled, what a sight!
A game of tag in morning light.
Branches stretching in silly twirls,
Daring raindrops, giving them swirls.

In this garden, joy's the crown,
With every shade, we wear a gown.
A merry band of blooms and fuzz,
Planting giggles, just because!

Anthem of the Youthful Canopy

Beneath the sun, a leafy choir,
Voices rise, a funny fire.
Chirpy songs from beaky friend,
On nature's notes, they all depend.

Twisting trunks in silly poses,
Tickling bees and playful roses.
A cloud floats by, they wave and cheer,
'Hey, fluffy friend, come join us here!'

Through a tangle of vines they swing,
Creating laughter, what fun they bring!
With each new sprout, a giggle grows,
In this wacky forest, anything goes!

A breeze comes by, it blows a tune,
Dancing daisies, under the moon.
In leafy hats, they sing out loud,
A merry jamboree, life's a crowd!

The Trail of the Tiny Vine

Along the path, a vine does prance,
In a floppy hat, it leads the dance.
With each small leaf, a step takes flight,
Twisting around with pure delight.

It tags a snail, oh what a chase,
They bump and laugh, a funny race.
A spider joins with a tiny jig,
They twirl and glide, not a single dig.

Sticky blooms wave hello in glee,
Ticklish petals on a merry spree.
The sun beams down, with laughter bright,
Celebrating life, oh what a sight!

At the end of the row, a feast is spread,
And all the bugs dance on the bread.
In this small world, fun never ends,
As giggling plants make silly friends!

Dreaming Among the Petals

In a splash of color, dreams take flight,
Butterflies giggle, oh what a sight.
Petals whisper secrets, soft and sweet,
A game of tag at the flower's feet.

Bumblebees buzz, a cheeky hum,
To the rhythm of nature's funny drum.
A cuckoo calls, tickling the day,
Flipping over petals, come out to play!

Sunshine glimmers through leafy lace,
Wacky shapes in a sunny embrace.
The daisies twist in wobbly glee,
"I'm funnier than you!" they declare with glee.

As twilight comes, they cuddle tight,
Under stars, they share their light.
Nighttime songs of joy unfold,
In whimsical dreams, their tales are told!

Whispers of the Young Tree

In a pot, I stand so tall,
With my leaves, I have a ball.
Swaying gently in the breeze,
I giggle at the buzzing bees.

Roots are tickled by the worms,
I dance around, oh how it squirms!
My neighbors, flowers, share a laugh,
As I stretch out my little staff.

Sunshine beams, I'm soaking it all,
Trying hard not to fall.
A squirrel rushes up to tease,
"Do you think you're tall as trees?"

In this garden, I feel grand,
Imitating a rock band!
With every breeze and playful sway,
I sing aloud all through the day.

Lullaby of Green Growth

Listen close, I hum a tune,
Bouncing leaves beneath the moon.
In my dreams, I grow so wide,
With mushrooms dancing by my side.

Each raindrop's like a little kiss,
Whispering, "Grow, you won't miss!"
I juggle seeds with reckless glee,
And hope to sprout my destiny.

A hungry bug came for a snack,
So I told him, "Hey, get back!
You'll make my shine a little dull,
I'm not a salad bowl for all!"

With every storm that comes my way,
I simply laugh, and shout, "Hooray!"
For with each splash and leafy shout,
I grow a little, without a doubt.

Renewal in the Breeze

Spring has come, I twirl and spin,
Dancing in my leafy skin.
The wind plays tricks, it pulls my hair,
I giggle, floating without a care.

Bumblebees buzz without a clue,
They keep mistaking me for blue!
But I just laugh, and play along,
A kid at heart, I hum my song.

With every gust, I sway and bend,
Making up jokes with every friend.
A raindrop says, "You look so green!"
I wink, "And shiny like a queen!"

Here in my patch, it's quite the show,
With leaf confetti, scattering low.
I'll grow a bit, sprout day by day,
And dance again when skies are gray.

Melody of Tender Shoots

My roots tickle in the dirt,
Feeling playful, never hurt.
Sunshine warms my cheeky grin,
As bugs do cartwheels on my skin.

Little leaves, we're full of cheer,
Swaying gently, far and near.
With a twist and a silly shimmy,
We'd make old oaks feel quite skinny.

I sing to clouds, both big and puffy,
Can't help but laugh when they get stuffy.
"Hey, drop some rain, if you're so bold,
Let's make a puddle – that'd be gold!"

So here I stand, proud and bright,
Making the garden feel just right.
Every day, I stretch and sing,
Creating joy, oh what a fling!

Rhythms of the Established Roots

In the garden where weeds dance,
A tiny sprout takes a chance.
With roots that giggle underground,
It's the silliest sight around.

The sun shines bright on its head,
It dreams of being a flower bed.
But all the bugs laugh and tease,
"You'll never outgrow your funny knees!"

A breeze comes by with a cheer,
"Don't worry, buddy, spring is near!"
Soon you'll spread leaves wide and tall,
And stomp on pests like a verdant ball.

So sway and twist in the sun,
Your leafy life has just begun.
With every giggle, laugh, and toot,
You'll rise and dance in your green suit!

Gleam of Dawn in Every Leaf

Every morning, dew drops twirl,
On a leaf that gives a twirl.
It sparkles and it wakes up slow,
Jumping up, 'Look at me, I glow!'

The air is filled with a bug parade,
With ladybugs dressed in their jade.
They sit and gossip on a branch,
As bees do awkward little dances.

Sunlight tickles the tips of grass,
And everyone gives a playful pass.
They laugh as worms slip and slide,
A comedy show playing outside.

Each blade whispers jokes and puns,
While ants march in their little runs.
Nature's laughter fills the field,
In every leaf, joy is revealed!

Flourish of the Verdant Dawn

A sprout in a pot looks around,
Says, "I really want to be renowned!"
With dreams of fame, it plans a show,
To prove it's the star of the grow.

The sun peeks in with a bright grin,
"You gotta stretch, my little kin!"
So it grows arms wide open wide,
Swaying to the rhythms of pride.

With friends like daisies all around,
They form a band without a sound.
Rocks tap dance, and ants join in,
As petals sway, twirling to win!

So here's to the blossoms in bloom,
With humor that fills every room.
Let's laugh and grow, come what may,
In this garden of joy, we'll play all day!

The Awakening Grove

In a grove where laughter's found,
Trees with grins abound, profound.
They tell each other funny tales,
Of how they dodged the winter gales.

Branches wave like happy hands,
Inviting all to join their bands.
Squirrels jive, and birds do loops,
While mushrooms form their dancing troops.

The breeze tickles with a tease,
As leaves burst forth with playful ease.
With every rustle, there's a cheer,
Join us now, the fun is here!

So let the roots hum their delight,
In this grove, everything feels right.
Nature's punchlines are on repeat,
With every sunrise, life's a treat!

The Birth of Woodland Dreams

In the pot, a sprout with flair,
Dreams of dancing in the air.
Singing songs from a tiny leaf,
Wishing for a life so brief.

This little green, a jokester bold,
Whispers tales of the trees so old.
Poking fun at passing bees,
Dare to climb and sway with ease.

Telling stories of the breeze,
While tickling the toes of trees.
With roots of mischief and glee,
It shimmies like a leaf on spree.

Oh, the dreams that seedlings weave,
Such a sight, you won't believe!
In woodland's realm, they take a stand,
Each sprout a star in leafy band.

Treetop Overture

Up high where the whispers soar,
A tiny tree begins to roar.
With a giggle and a wink,
It dances on the edge of pink.

Leaves shake hands with clouds above,
In this treetop tale of love.
Squirrels roll their eyes and grin,
At the bouncing bark within.

A sunbeam shines, a spotlight bright,
As branches sway with sheer delight.
Bouncing, leaping, oh what fun,
Nature's chatter has just begun!

With every breeze, the branches play,
A symphony of green ballet.
Come and join the laughter loud,
In the shade, we dance and crowd.

Unfurling Under the Sun

Watch me stretch, I'm feeling grand,
With leaves that twirl, oh isn't it planned?
A tiny bone, but dreams so wide,
Like a tree with a playful stride.

Sun-kissed petals sneak a peek,
While ants parade like they're unique.
I laugh at clouds, they look so slow,
As I wiggle in this bright glow.

With roots entwined in the playful earth,
Every flicker feels like mirth.
"Hey there, flower!" I shout aloud,
"Join my fun, let's make it loud!"

Unfurling leaves, a vivid scene,
In this garden of evergreen.
Each day, a story just begun,
With mirth and magic in the sun.

Songs of Life in the Soil

Down below, the critters sing,
Life is bustling under spring.
Roots are tapping a happy beat,
Till worms dance in their earthy seat.

Seeds are having a wild chat,
"Who's the tallest? Can you beat that?"
They giggle as they grow and sway,
In a contest of the fun-filled way.

Microbes throw a funky show,
Spinning tales of seeds aglow.
With little duets, they take a dive,
In the rich soil, they feel alive.

Every gust brings a new surprise,
As life blooms large before our eyes.
Nature's jesters, each tiny friend,
In this kingdom where fun won't end.

Hymn of the First Green Thumb

In the garden I plant my dreams,
Tiny seeds that giggle and scream.
Worms throw parties, dirt's their glue,
Dance all night 'til the morning dew.

A sunflower's laughing, as tall as my head,
Tickles my nose, 'I need some bread!'
But all I offer is a shade of glee,
'Grow, dear plants, and just hang with me!'

The daisies joke, 'We're gourmet delights!'
While ants march like they're on great flights.
A carrot whispers, 'I'm no bystander!'
'Let's root for fun, not just for the planter!'

And in this patch, wild giggles abound,
Nature's jokesters spin joy all around.
With every sprout, a chuckle's reborn,
In this jolly jungle, I feel adorned.

Awakened Harmony of Nature's Children

A butterfly flutters, a comic ballet,
Sipping sweet nectar, come join the fray!
The flowers clap hands, they twist and sway,
'This garden's our stage, come dance, come play!'

The sunbeams giggle, casting warm tints,
As squirrels hurl acorns, they're nature's clints.
Rabbits with antics, what a flashy show!
In the theater of greens, we steal the glow.

Trees elbow each other, they whisper with cheer,
'Look at those ants, like they've had too much beer!'
Petals burst laughter, in colors they glow,
'Join us, dear breeze, let your joy freely flow!'

And when the moon rises, the dreamers unite,
Under starlit covers, we giggle all night.
Nature's children laugh, a merry parade,
In this lush world, no worries invade.

The Fresh Start of the Verdant Path

Awake with a chuckle, today's a fresh start,
Tiny sprouts laughing, they're full of heart.
A beetle runs past me, with shoes far too big,
'Tis a funny old dance, oh what a wig!'

The grass sways gently, a carpet of glee,
Rolling with laughter, so carefree.
Every worm in the soil, sings a low tune,
While crickets are comedians, croaking at noon.

The daisies chime in with a rascally grin,
'What's cooler than flowers? We're winning, let's spin!'
The fern plays piano, the leaves keep the beat,
Under a canopy where sun and fun meet.

So let's waltz through the garden, with giggles galore,
Embracing the quirk of this green-sprouting lore.
With every joyful petal, every crooked vine,
Nature's laughter echoes, a sweet, funny sign.

Nature's Early Symphony

In dawn's tender light, the band starts to play,
A cacophony of chirps, quite charmingly gay.
Bees buzz their tunes while frogs croak in time,
Off-beat but groovy, that's nature's rhyme!

The trees shake their leaves, a rhythmic ballet,
While shadows and sunlight play peek-a-boo sway.
A chatty old crow, in a symphonic mood,
Caws out loud, in a comedic brood.

The flowers pop open, with a colorful cheer,
'Join our orchestra, come lend us your ear!'
The breeze fluffs the notes, rising high to the sky,
With laughter and giggles, they float carelessly by.

As dusk starts to hum, the crickets take flight,
In this orchestra of greens, we dance through the night.
Nature's early symphony, a joyous delight,
Sings of fun and laughter, under the starlight.

Melodies of the Growing Woods

In a forest full of giggles,
A tiny sprout does sway,
With whispers from the breezes,
It dances night and day.

The acorns drop in laughter,
They bounce and roll away,
The mushrooms join the jester,
As critters start to play.

Each branch stretches like a yawn,
The leaves are tickled green,
A symphony of nature,
With silliness unseen.

So listen to the rustle,
As branches play along,
In the harmonious shuffle,
Of this woodland song.

The Sun-Kissed Lullaby

Underneath a bright blue sky,
A wobbly shoot will sway,
With a grin it tries to fly,
And giggles come to play.

The clouds wear silly hats,
In puffs of cotton cheer,
While raindrops dance like cats,
And tickle as they near.

A chorus of chirping birds,
Sing jokes upon the breeze,
They flap their wings in herds,
As branches sway with ease.

In every beam of sunshine,
A wink from leaves so bright,
They sway in silly rhythms,
From morning until night.

The Radiant Crescendo of Youth

Little roots are snoozing tight,
While dreaming of a height,
They wrinkle up their noses,
And giggle at their plight.

The bugs are hosting parties,
With confetti made of dust,
They dance upon the branches,
In laughter, free and just.

Blades of grass play hide and seek,
With daisies in a line,
As whispers turn to tickles,
In soft sunlight divine.

So here's to every sprout,
Who dreams of growing tall,
With funny friends about,
To catch them when they fall.

The Tree of Tomorrow's Hope

A sprout with big ambitions,
Wants to be a giant tree,
With branches full of dreams,
And giggles wild and free.

Each leaf a little jester,
Dressed in shades of bright green,
They laugh at every raindrop,
In nature's funny scene.

The roots have ticklish tickles,
They hide beneath the ground,
Chasing bugs and cooking plans,
In every wiggle found.

The sun will shine tomorrow,
With joy that's hard to cope,
A story made of laughter,
That whispers tales of hope.

Soundtrack of Spring's Awakening

A little sprout inside the ground,
Dances about without a sound.
It wiggles and jigs in the sun's warm glow,
Laughing at winter's heavy snow.

Tiny leaves wave like jazz hands,
While raindrops play their rhythm bands.
Bees buzzing in their silly way,
Join in the fun to greet the day.

The grass is tapping its little toes,
As daffodils put on botanical shows.
Oh, how nature loves to play,
In this vibrant, green ballet!

With each stretch and every leap,
The little plants don't dare to sleep.
They shimmy and shake, so full of cheer,
Glad to see spring has finally here!

The Hopeful Anthem of New Growth

A seedling sprouts with hopeful glee,
Singing its tune for all to see.
"Look at me, I'm really tall!"
It teases with a giggle, oh what a ball!

The worms join in with wiggly cheer,
As butterflies flutter, spreading cheer.
"Hey, little bud, will you bloom soon?"
It replies, "Under this bright, big moon!"

The sun shines down with a wink and grin,
It knows the fun is about to begin.
The sprout sways like a festive drum,
Ready to welcome springtime's hum!

Buds pop open with laughter and song,
Nature's crew now feels so strong.
Together they dance, this merry crew,
Oh, what joy in life anew!

Rhythms of the Blushing Blossom

A bud blinks awake, a curious sight,
Winking at ants with pure delight.
"I'm coming out, hold your applause!"
It shimmies and shakes, without a pause.

Petals unfurl like a royal cape,
Creating quite the floral shape.
"Don't crowd me, bees, I can't take it!"
The budding bloom throws a tiny fit.

With every breeze, it tosses and twirls,
As ladybugs giggle and whirl.
"Blush a little brighter!" the daisies sing,
The garden laughs at the joy of spring.

In this colorful garden parade,
Flora and fauna come out to play.
Each flower beams in the warming sun,
A fantastic show, oh what fun!

Crescendo in the Canopy

A tree stands tall, with branches wide,
Swaying gently, a joyful ride.
"Hey, look at me, I'm really cool!"
It boasts to birds in its leafy school.

Leaves rustle like giggles in the air,
"This is our show, come join us there!"
Squirrels jump in a playful duel,
"Who can climb higher? What a great rule!"

The breeze carries melodies sweet,
As critters tap dance with nimble feet.
"Swing to the left, then twirl with flair!"
The tree giggles, spreading joy everywhere.

Under the boughs, laughter surrounds,
Nature's chorus sings joyful sounds.
In this grand show, life finds a way,
A celebration of each bright day!

The Original Tune of Nature's Children

Little leaves dance in the breeze,
Swaying happily with such ease.
A twig stands up, tries to prance,
But falls again—no second chance!

The flowers chat with buzzing bees,
While ants march by with perfect ease.
Each acorn dreams of growing tall,
But first, they play a game of ball!

The sun peeks in, a cheeky tease,
As shade runs off, saying, "Mind your fleece!"
Roots underground are telling jokes,
While squirrels giggle at the folks.

Green friends gather to sing out loud,
Mushrooms pop up, feeling proud.
Nature's kids, in joyful cheer,
Are cracking up from ear to ear!

A Symphony of Sunlit Inspiration

In the morning, the sun does rise,
Casting shadows—oh, what a surprise!
A caterpillar struts with flair,
While a ladybug fixes her hair.

Bamboo plays a xylophone beat,
As critters stomp their tiny feet.
A chorus of chirps fills the air,
While rabbits swirl, without a care.

Just then, a breeze, a gentle nudge,
Causes all the flowers to judge.
"Who wore it best?" they giggle and squeal,
Petals flutter, it's a big deal!

The trees all sway like they're in sync,
While the grass performs its lively clink.
In this funny concert of rhyme,
Nature's laughter transcends all time!

Notes from the Canopy of Life

Up high, the branches take the lead,
Whispering secrets, oh indeed!
A parrot jokes, a few birds laugh,
While squirrels act as nature's staff.

Leaves play tag with the warm spring air,
As fluff clouds drift without a care.
A woodpecker's on a non-stop quest,
Knocking tunes on trees—such zest!

Roots interlock, forming a band,
Sharing stories, oh so grand.
The sun and moon share playful glares,
As crickets dance without their cares.

With every breeze, a melody flows,
Tickling toes, where laughter grows.
Nature's symphony, a wondrous song,
A silly place where all belong!

The Whispers of Awakening Earth

In the early light, the ground's a stage,
Worms wiggle, filled with glee and rage.
A tiny sprout gives a lilting shout,
"Here I come! Look out, no doubt!"

Mud pies fly, oh what a sight,
As we gather, sharing delight.
The sunbeams laugh, tickling the ground,
While daisies twirl, spinning round!

The raindrops tap—a percussive beat,
As puddles form, a playground sweet.
A lizard cracks a silly grin,
Joining in, with a funky spin.

With each new day, the earth awakes,
Joking around with sunny breaks.
Nature's humor, a joyful mirth,
In every corner of our dear earth!

Anthem of the Arising Canopy

In the morning light, little leaves dance,
Chasing the breezes, giggle at chance.
Roots play tag with worms beneath,
While the sun peeks in with a golden wreath.

Branches stretch wide, a hide-and-seek game,
Squirrels jump in, but who can name?
The blossoms that nod their heads in cheer,
Whispering secrets only they hear.

Bumblebees buzzing, a comedic band,
Drumming on petals with a wobbly hand.
Clouds drift by, acting shy above,
What a hilarious dance, a nature's love!

Oh, watch the shadows play on the ground,
As playful critters swirl all around.
With laughter and joy, the forest thrives,
In this wild concert, where humor survives.

Swaying to Life's Cadence

In the meadow wild, the tall grass sways,
Tickling the ankles in whimsical ways.
The caterpillar's wiggle, oh what a sight,
Grooving to rhythms of day and night.

Crickets chirp jokes in the pale moonlight,
Hopping to the beat, causing quite a fright.
Fireflies flash, with a wink and a grin,
Lighting up paths, where the fun will begin.

Dandelions bob, like little heads of gold,
Telling tall tales of adventures bold.
The breeze takes a turn, with a playful twirl,
And suddenly, whoosh!—there goes a swirl!

As the trees chuckle, their limbs intertwine,
Nature's own dance, a majestic design.
In this merry ballet, where spirits uplift,
Joy is the treasure, the world's best gift.

A Whisper Among the Woods

Deep in the woods, a soft chuckle flows,
A mossy bench winks under the snows.
The owls share riddles, perched with delight,
While squirrels throw acorns, oh, what a sight!

Tiny mushrooms laugh as the raindrops drop,
Bouncing in puddles, they just can't stop.
A raccoon in a hat, looking quite sly,
Dances with shadows that flit by.

Listen closely now, to the leaves' bright chime,
They gossip of weather and the silliest time.
Each twig a storyteller, with tales to unfold,
Of mishaps and giggles in the crisp, cool hold.

When breezes tickle the branches with glee,
Nature's own laughter is wild and free.
A symphony of joy brewed under the wood,
In a world full of whimsy, where everything's good.

Nature's Silent Crescendo

In a garden bright, the daisies compose,
A cheerful tune that everyone knows.
They sway in a rhythm, petals out wide,
While the bees spin about, full of pride.

The tomatoes are red, flaunting their flair,
Arguing with carrots who simply don't care.
A lettuce giggles, the onions all smirk,
Creating a harmony where veggies lurk.

Then comes the wind, with a whoosh and a swish,
Twirling the flowers, fulfilling their wish.
Clouds puff up, trying to join in,
While the raindrops fall, a new dance to begin.

As the sun sets low, the stars pop awake,
Eager to join the joy we partake.
Nature's concert, a medley so sweet,
Where laughter and life meet in incredible beat.

The Rhapsody of the Budding Horizon

In the garden, there's a dance,
Tiny leaves in leafy pants.
Twisting, turning, sprouting free,
Who knew plants could be so zany?

In the morning, they all cheer,
Whispering secrets to the ear.
They giggle softly in the breeze,
Calling friends, come plant some trees!

Worms are twirling, soil does sway,
"Hey, don't eat my roots today!"
Meanwhile, sunbeams play charades,
Shining bright on leafy blades.

So if you wander past my patch,
Prepare for leafy jokes to catch.
A garden glee, a joyful jest,
Nature's humor, we're truly blessed.

Melodies from a Sunlit Corner

In the corner, sunflowers sway,
Chasing rays throughout the day.
"Look at me!" one proudly yells,
While dancing with its petal pals.

Bees are buzzing, what a sound!
As they bounce all around.
"Can you keep up?" they seem to chime,
Wings a-flutter, what a rhyme!

A squirrel scampers, what a sight!
Stealing seeds with all its might.
"Hey, that's mine!" the plants will shout,
As Mr. Squirrel twirls about.

With laughter in the evening hue,
They whisper jokes on skies so blue.
A garden's giggle, pure delight,
When sunlit corners blaze so bright.

The Fantasia of Fresh Sprouts

Little sprouts with dreams so grand,
Peek from soil, oh, isn't it planned?
They throw a party, gather round,
With tiny hats, all tightly bound.

"Hey there, friend, let's stretch and grow,
Who knew the soil would be our show?"
They wiggle roots and dance in place,
Sporting smiles on every face!

A rabbit hops, a curious guest,
"Mind if I join your leafy fest?"
But sprouts just giggle, shake their heads,
"Sorry, buddy, go munch your bread!"

With laughter swirling beneath the sun,
They sway and hum, oh, what fun!
Nature's whimsy, never a bore,
Come join our rooty, zany chore!

Nature's Prelude to Autumn

As autumn whispers, leaves turn gold,
The plants prepare to break the mold.
"Time for sweaters, leaves, don your gear!"
A giggling chorus, loud and clear!

Squirrels stash snacks, how bizarre!
"Is this a feast or a scavenger star?"
Each nut's a treasure for winter's chill,
With furry friends running wild at will.

Pumpkins roll in, all round and bright,
"Watch out, I'm here and full of fright!"
They bounce and laugh, a comical sight,
As autumn's grace takes flight in delight.

So raise a glass to seasons' shift,
Nature's punny, playful gift.
With mirth and cheer, we'll sing along,
To this funny twist, our hearts belong!

Serenade of the Budding Branches

In a world of green and glee,
Little buds sway, so carefree.
Dancing gently in the breeze,
Whispering secrets to the trees.

With a wiggle and a twist,
They form a leafy, joyful list.
Branches giggle, roots tap dance,
Nature's folly, given a chance.

Buds in bloom, a comedic show,
They tickle leaves as they grow.
A frolic with polka dots,
Nature's humor hits the spots!

The sun winks and the rain claps,
Every droplet, a little slap.
Amongst the laughter, they declare,
"Let's grow upwards without a care!"

The Gentle Rise of Nature

A sprout pops up, it sees the light,
With a grin, it springs with might.
Feeling silly, it stretches wide,
Trying hard to take in pride.

Petals giggle as they bloom,
"Look at us, we're all in costume!"
Sunshine flashes, oh what fun,
The garden's party has begun!

Grasshoppers chirp a funny tune,
While blossoms dance beneath the moon.
Nature's laughter fills the air,
A joyous hint is everywhere!

Every droplet has a joke,
Tickling leaves, a light-hearted poke.
Nature's rise, so gentle, true,
Always brings out the silly in you.

Tuning into Nature's Aria

In the woods, a concert starts,
Little leaves play funky parts.
Each twig strums on its own string,
While flowers join in, sweetly sing.

A bumblebee beats the drum,
Making sure everyone's having fun.
Hopping frogs join in the cheer,
Their croaks a sound that's crystal clear!

Branches sway with pure delight,
Grinding roots dance through the night.
Nature's band keeps the beat,
With every laugh, they're hard to beat!

As the sunrise starts to gleam,
They gather 'round, a vibrant team.
A show of folly all around,
Nature's humor knows no bound.

The Pulse of New Beginnings

Tiny shoots from the ground pop,
Bouncing high like they can't stop.
They laugh and sing, a raucous bunch,
Munching leaves for a morning crunch!

With each stretch, they tease the sun,
Claiming victory — they have won!
Frogs in hats cheer from the side,
Rooting for their friends with pride.

As rainclouds form a jolly troupe,
Droplets join in, a playful loop.
Nature's pulse, a vibrant beat,
Makes every moment feel so sweet!

The world wakes up, all bright and new,
With every giggle, a fresh view.
In this dance of life, they thrive,
With a chuckle, they come alive!

An Infant's Dance in the Meadow

In the meadow with sunshine bright,
A giggling sprout takes its flight.
Wobbling joy in the gentle breeze,
It dances with ants, oh, what a tease!

Bouncing around like a tiny ball,
It sways and slips — oh, what a fall!
Around it flies a lazy bee,
Buzzing along, full of glee.

Every blade of grass joins the fun,
Twirling together under the sun.
The whole field grins at the little one's cheer,
Laughter echoing, lively and clear!

As the sun sets, it starts to sway,
Humming a tune for the end of play.
With dreams of dancing till break of dawn,
Little sprout laughs, "Pick me up, come on!"

A Treetop's Jubilant Rise

Up high in the sky, a tree takes a bow,
Reaching for clouds with a playful vow.
Branches outstretched, they wiggle and cheer,
"Look, I'm taller than squirrels this year!"

Leaves rustle softly, like tickles of air,
"Hey, look at me, I'm not going anywhere!"
Twisting and twirling, the trunk stands so proud,
It winks at the sun, "I'm part of the crowd!"

A bird lands nearby, with a smile and a song,
"Join me, dear tree, let's dance along!"
With every sway, the branches take flight,
Creating a ruckus from morning to night!

When breezes come calling, they shout with delight,
Treetop giggles fill the warm, soft night.
In the heart of the forest, a party's awake,
Where trees laugh and dance, and no one will quake!

Resonance of Resilient Roots

Deep in the earth where the roots are found,
They chat and they giggle, all safe underground.
"Hey, did you hear? They want us to grow!
Let's send a tickle up to the show!"

Wiggling and jiggling, they twist and they turn,
"Let's reach for the sky, it's our time to learn!"
They whisper in harmony, a cheeky little crew,
"Who says we can't have a laugh or two?"

As the sap starts to flow, they plot their huge rise,
Each one a comedian in leafy disguise.
"Let's stretch our limbs; oh, don't you feel spry?
And if we get pruned, let's just wave bye-bye!"

With roots full of wisdom and quirks to impart,
They dig in their heels and say, "Let's depart!"
Together they rumble, a soft, playful sigh,
"Oh, look at us now! We're the best, oh so spry!"

Chime of the Practices of Growth

Tap-tap-tap, a rhythm begins,
Tiny seeds giggle; the fun never thins.
"Let's stretch and let's wiggle; let's throw our hands high!

We're destined for greatness, just watch us all fly!"

With sunshine and raindrops, a jolly parade,
Nature's own circus, life's grand escapade.
"Who knew that growing could tickle so much?
We're the stars of the garden, the plants with a touch!"

They chime and they jingle, like a band on the floor,
Each leaf a musician, oh, who asked for more?
A twig plays the drums, while branches sway to the beat,
Together they giggle, such a funny feat!

At dusk they all gather, their laughter entwined,
In the heart of the garden, joyfully aligned.
"Here's to the practices of fun and of cheer,
We'll grow and we'll joke, for another bright year!"

The Radiance of New Beginnings

Little green shoots so spry,
Dancing under the bright blue sky.
They giggle with the buzzing bees,
Tickling leaves in the gentle breeze.

Sunshine paints their cheeky grin,
While worms applaud with a little spin.
"Grow up fast!" the flowers shout,
But the saplings laugh and wiggle about.

With raindrops flicking like nimble feet,
They splish and splash, oh so sweet!
Planting dreams in playful rows,
Chasing clouds as the garden grows.

So here's to laughs in the soil so proud,
Where roots hide secrets, soft and loud.
In the light's embrace, they sing and sway,
Funny little sprouts, brightening the day!

A Messenger's Whisper Among the Groves

In the shade where laughter flutters,
Branches chatter, leaves in mutters.
A squirrel's tale, a joke well-told,
About acorns wearing crowns of gold.

Through the trees a riddle flies,
"Have you tried to wear the skies?"
As critters giggle, twitching their tails,
While the breeze dances with quirky gales.

A message sent by fluffy clouds,
Tickling the earth in happy shrouds.
With whispers that tickle the roots below,
The woodland chuckles, putting on a show.

So listen close when springtime comes,
For frolics hide where the laughter hums.
In every grove, where friendships thrive,
The merriest tales of trees come alive!

The Rise of the Blossoming Heart

From tiny seeds to leafy charms,
A budding heart with open arms.
It shimmies bright in leafy cheer,
Wishing on starlight, drinking in beer.

Every bloom a giggly jest,
"I'm more colorful than all the rest!"
Petals flapping like silly hands,
Tickling the wind, in joyous bands.

So come and twirl in the sun's warm glow,
Where blossoms share their funny show.
With laughter loud, and colors bold,
Their stories weave as spring unfolds.

In the garden, the hearts take flight,
A riot of colors, a pure delight.
With every laugh, their spirits grow,
In the dance of flowers, love on show!

Ballad of the Budding Treetop

High above, where dreams take wing,
A budding treetop starts to sing.
With acorns bouncing and giggles bright,
It sways with joy, a whimsical sight.

The branches twist in a playful dance,
While squirrels join in the carefree prance.
"Oh look at me!" the treetop beams,
"I'm the most delightful of all the dreams!"

With chirpy friends in a happy spree,
They build a nest of giggles and glee.
The sun peeks in with a winking grin,
As laughter echoes, where fun begins.

So raise a toast to the playful boughs,
As they twist and twirl in nature's vows.
For in this canopy of silly delight,
The world grows brighter, oh what a sight!

Chorus of the Verdant Awakening

In a pot, a seedling sways,
Telling tales of sunny days.
With leaves like arms, it starts to jig,
Wobbling round, oh so big!

It dreams of roots in deep, rich earth,
Imagining its verdant birth.
A dancing sprout with silly flair,
Tickling worms who stop and stare!

Chasing bugs that tickle toes,
Giggling as the garden grows.
With every breeze, they twist and cheer,
Welcome spring, our laughter here!

So come and join this leafy ball,
Twirl and spin, let's have a ball!
In this green realm, we all belong,
Join the chorus, sing along!

New Growth in the Dance of Seasons

Tiny shoots against the frost,
Hopping up, they're never lost.
A leaf does a pirouette,
With each turn, it laughs and sweats!

Raindrops tap a happy beat,
Dancing with those little feet.
Each flower twirls in bright array,
Joining in the grand ballet!

Nuts and acorns make a fuss,
Rolling round without a bus.
They tumble down, they take a dive,
In this party, we're alive!

Oh, the sun beams down with glee,
As all the sprouts play hide and seek.
With every glance, a wink, a grin,
The season's dance will always win!

Song of the Tender Shoots

Little sprouts stretch out their toes,
Napping where the sunshine glows.
They burp and yawn, then leap on high,
Reaching to tickle the sky!

With every breeze, they giggle loud,
Like silly kids in a happy crowd.
"A caterpillar joined the fun,
He rolls with laughter, oh what a run!"

Jumpy buds with petals bright,
Poking fun at bees in flight.
They steal the nectar, what a show,
"Hey, come back! We want some too!"

So let's cheer for every sprout,
Dancing free, they twist about.
In gardens wide, their joy persists,
Mocking clouds, the sun insists!

Notes of the Flourishing Glade

In a glade where giggles bloom,
Tiny trees find lots of room.
With twigs and leaves, they play with glee,
Singing tunes from A to Z!

The mushrooms clap as ferns do bow,
"Take a seat, we need a show now!"
With leafy hats and silly shoes,
They stomp the ground with jolly blues.

Squirrels dance with acorn hats,
Jumping high to outsmart chats.
A funny frog joins in delight,
Croaks a beat, and hugs the night!

So dance along, oh friends so dear,
In this glade, there's nothing to fear.
With every leaf, we twirl and sing,
In joy, we find our springtime zing!

Nature's Gentle Nursery Rhyme

In the garden, plants take a stand,
With roots below and leaves so grand.
They wiggle and giggle, sun on their face,
A leafy parade in a green-trimmed place.

The daisies are chatting, the roses are proud,
While the sunflowers dance, attracting a crowd.
A carrot sneezes, a tomato slips,
All join in laughter, with joyful quips.

The worms are the dancers, in soil they groove,
While bumblebees buzz, their bodies to move.
With petals all fluttering, what a sight!
Nature's own party, from morning to night.

So here's to the plants, the clowns of the earth,
Each leaf tells a story, each twig shows its worth.
With roots down steady and branches so spry,
Let's sing to the garden, oh my, oh my!

Serenade of the Budding Branch

A branch starts to quiver, oh what could it be?
It thinks of a dance, with a leaf as its spree.
The squirrels sneak peeking, paws all a-clap,
While birds pull a number, from up on a sap.

The breeze is a tickler, it sways to and fro,
With chirps from the robins that steal the show.
A little green bud chuckles, its first view so bright,
Enjoying the chaos twixt morning and night.

A butterfly flutters, a thief of the scene,
Stealing the nectar and making it clean.
Yet the bud just giggles and plays with the breeze,
"Come join us, dear friends, let's shake with the trees!"

So here's to the branches, so silly and spry,
In every green giggle, we find joy nearby.
With leaves laugh-out-loud and roots deeply planted,
Nature's own humor, forever enchanted!

Chant of the Emerging Bloom

A flower yawned wide, stretching under the sun,
"Wake up, sleepy petals, our party's begun!"
With colors a-blossom, oh such a fine sight,
They twirl in the garden, what a pure delight!

A daffodil danced, with a twist and a spin,
While tulips around her joined in with a grin.
The daisies sang loud, in a chorus so sweet,
With laughter and petals, they all tap their feet.

Occasionally sneezing, a flower might go,
A tickle from pollen, oh no, not the show!
But laughter erupts; they can't help but thrive,
In the warmth of the sun, oh they feel so alive!

So let's raise a glass to the blooms in the field,
Their humor is timeless, and their joy is revealed.
With colors and giggles in nature's grand scheme,
Let's dance with the flowers and wake from the dream!

The Tulip's First Tune

With a bud that is bold and a stem full of grace,
A tulip proclaimed, "I'll take center space!"
It swayed with the wind, in a shirt of bright hue,
"Come join my fine fable, I'll sing just for you!"

A bee buzzed on over, mischief in tow,
But the tulip just laughed, "You won't steal my show!"
With petals like slippers, it twirled all around,
While ladybugs clapped, sharing joy that they found.

The sun dropped a wink, as it chortled away,
While the tulip grew cheeky, in playful display.
"Let's tango, my friends, let's make this a ball!"
With laughter and giggles, from springtime to fall.

So here's to the tulip, with humor so bright,
In the heart of the bloom, where joy takes its flight.
With each little chuckle, new stories are spun,
In the fairest of gardens, where all life is fun!

Chorus of the Tender Sprout

In a garden full of glee,
Little sprout is dancing free.
With a wiggle and a twist,
It won't to be dismissed!

Sunny rays tap on its head,
"Grow up straight!" the winds have said.
But it giggles with delight,
And leans left just for spite.

Raindrops tickle as they fall,
"Hey, look at me!" it starts to call.
A tiny leaf waves in the air,
Joyful choir everywhere!

Roots are grinning in the ground,
They're the best pals it has found.
Together they sway and play,
In their funny little way.

Lullaby for a Growing Tree

In the dusk, a cradle sways,
Breezes whisper soft, amused plays.
"Hush now, leaf, don't take a peek,
Dream of sunshine, it's not bleak!"

Branches yawn, they stretch out wide,
But sleepy buds begin to hide.
Worms are giggling at the scene,
"Oh, how funny this can be!"

Boughs are snoring, oh so sweet,
Lullabies beneath their feet.
And in the moon's bright glow,
The dirtlings dance, putting on a show!

When the dawn begins to spark,
Tiny cracks, it leaves a mark.
Off it giggles, a sprouty spree,
A dance party for all to see!

Harmonies of the Fresh Bud

A bud appears, so sprightly bright,
Singing tunes from morning light.
With a wink and a playful twirl,
It initiates a floral whirl!

Bees are buzzing, taking cues,
Learning steps, they cannot lose!
Oh, the dance, a sight to share,
Pollen flying everywhere!

"Do the twist!" the petals shout,
"Bend your stems! There's no doubt!"
Laughter echoes through the dew,
It's a party, yes, it's true!

Underneath the sunny arch,
Roots are up for their own march.
They'll sway low, just like the sprout,
Making music without a doubt.

The Ballad of Into the Light

Little sprout peeks out, oh my!
It stretches up to kiss the sky.
"Hey, look at me, I'm on display!
I've got dreams that run and play!"

Twisting fun in sunlight's gaze,
Every moment, it will craze.
With a giggle and a sigh,
It spins around and tries to fly.

Clouds drift by, they share a grin,
Who knew growth could be this win?
Dance of limbs while shadows tease,
"Rise above!" with gentle ease.

Through the struggles, oh what fun,
Soon you'll bloom into the sun.
And when the day finally dips,
You'll share a laugh with all your tips.

The Joyful Dance of Every Bud

In a pot, the sprouts do sway,
Wiggling roots, come out to play.
With tiny hats of vibrant green,
They hold a party, quite the scene!

Sunshine giggles, rain joins in,
Each leaf twirls with a cheeky grin.
A beetle leads the happy waltz,
While ants perform their funky vaults!

Petals jump, and stems do spin,
Imagine the joy that lives within.
New buds whisper silly tricks,
In nature's dance, there are no kicks!

With every sway, they take their stance,
Tiny greens in a grand expanse.
A joyful dance, a leafy jest,
In the garden, life is blessed!

A Fresh Leaf's Silent Message

A fresh leaf held a secret style,
With veins that shimmered, made us smile.
It scribbled notes with drops of dew,
Creating art no one else knew!

The wind would giggle, twist and glide,
As messages danced on leafy pride.
"Look at me!" the green one spouts,
With not a care for tiny doubts!

It flutters softly in the breeze,
Whispering tales of silly sprees.
Each rustle chirps a vibrant tune,
Making all the flowers swoon!

So next you stroll down shady lanes,
Look for the leaves with quirky brains.
They'll share a laugh, a giggle or two,
In their quiet world of greenish hue!

Sweet Serenades of the Meadow

In the meadow, flowers sing,
A chorus led by buzzing fling.
Daisies twirl, while violets hum,
In a floral dance, oh so fun!

Grasshoppers play their jumping strings,
Bees join in, their sweetness brings.
Each petal's wink a laugh so light,
In the meadow, it feels so right!

Butterflies flutter, wearing flair,
Spreading joy, with love in air.
With every breeze, they wave and cheer,
In this meadow, bliss is near!

So if ever in need of glee,
Head to the blooms, sing wild and free.
For every bud that lifts its head,
Is filled with songs that love has spread!

The Dawn's Chorus Among the Branches

At dawn, the branches start to sing,
Warblers chirp, like bells that ring.
Squirrels laugh, as acorns drop,
While dewdrops glisten, a playful crop!

Each twig joins in, a silly tune,
Praising the bright, beaming moon.
With rustling leaves, and branches sway,
The morning warms, in a cheeky way!

A woodpecker taps, a percussion beat,
While the sunlight dances on tiny feet.
In the trees, a symphony grows,
Of silly songs that nature chose!

So next time dawn breaks bright and clear,
Listen close, let the magic steer.
In every croak and rustle found,
Is laughter held in nature's sound!

Euphony of the Emerging Flora

In the cranny of the earth, a sprout did dare,
Feeling the sun's warm giggles in the air.
Worms with tiny trumpets play a tune,
While seedlings wiggle, dancing to the moon.

A raindrop fell and splashed with glee,
Said, "Listen close, it's a jubilee!"
The buds all chuckled, sprightly and spry,
With roots that wagged as they waved goodbye.

The daisies told jokes with petals so bright,
Making the grass laugh, oh what a sight!
A beetle crooned ballads from the leaf,
As butterflies twirled in astonishing relief.

So here's a riddle from the garden's heart,
What blooms with laughter—well, that's the art!
Join in the frolic, and you'll surely see,
Nature's giggles—growing wild and free!

Aria of the Ascent

Up the stem, the whispers rise,
Pixies peek from leaf disguise.
A hearty laugh from bumblebee,
"Climb a bit higher, come dance with me!"

Chasing shadows, then in the light,
The flowers plan a wild kite flight.
Swaying gently on the breeze,
While ants in suits march with great ease.

"What's that sound?" cried little thyme,
"A tune from the mint, oh worth a rhyme!"
They twirled around, oh so sprightly,
Even the thorns smiled—slightly tightly.

So sing with me in this green ballet,
Where laughter grows bright every day.
From roots up high to skies so vast,
We'll belt out joy and hold it fast!

The Song of Soil and Sky

When humus hums and clouds collide,
A goofy dance begins to glide.
Earthworms tangle in a muddy twist,
While daisies gossip, they can't resist.

A mole pops up, wearing a grin,
"Oh stop the fuss, let the fun begin!"
The daisies whisper 'bout the sun's sweet rays,
Dancing around for several days.

With gnarled roots that tickle the ground,
A party starts with a rumble sound.
The soil sings while skies respond,
A symphony where all are fond.

So let's cheer with the grasses so spry,
For every sprout that dares to try.
In this duet of Earth and air,
We'll raise our voices, no need to scare!

Harmonizing with the Breeze

A gentle breeze, a cheeky tease,
Whispers secrets through the trees.
"What do you call a tree that sings?"
"Aspen-sational!" Oh how it rings!

Petals fluttered, they rolled with laughter,
Creating a tune that none could master.
A frolicsome flow from the lilacs flowed,
As sunshine chuckled, its warmth bestowed.

Tiny seeds took off in flight,
On an unexpected morning bright.
Their laughs echoed through tangled vines,
A perfect pitch of silly lines.

So join the chorus, delightful and grand,
With nature's symphony, let's take a stand.
Here in the garden of the plush and free,
We'll sing our anthem in harmony!

www.ingramcontent.com/pod-product-compliance
Lightning Source LLC
Chambersburg PA
CBHW071829160426
43209CB00003B/251